As
Action

By Emily Costello

CELEBRATION PRESS
Pearson Learning Group

Contents

Meet Jessica 3
What Is Asthma? 4
Asthma and Athletics 9
Living With Asthma 15
What the Future Holds 20
Glossary 24

Meet Jessica

This is Jessica. She attends school in Jersey City, New Jersey. She wants to try out for the school basketball team this fall.

Like nearly 5 million other American kids, Jessica has asthma [AZ mah]. The number of people with this disease is growing. Asthma is one of the most common reasons American children miss school or spend time in the hospital. Asthma has no cure, but doctors can help people with asthma live healthy lives.

Jessica doesn't let asthma get in the way of her basketball.

What is Asthma?

Asthma is a disease of the airways. People with asthma can have trouble breathing. They may also **wheeze** and cough.

When you breathe in, air travels down your windpipe through airways called **bronchial tubes** (BRAHN ke ehl toobz) and enters your lungs. In the lungs the bronchial tubes branch out to smaller and smaller tubes. At the very end are tiny air sacs called **alveoli** (al VEE oh lee). The alveoli help oxygen from the air you breathe enter the blood stream. Human beings could not live without oxygen.

Exercise is one of the main triggers of asthma.

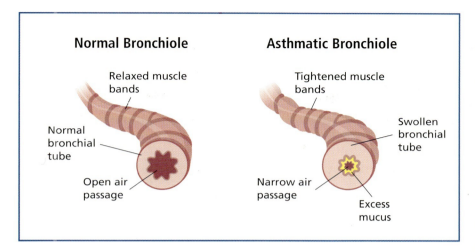

This diagram shows what happens to airways during an asthma attack.

For most people, breathing is easy. That's not always true for **asthmatics**, or people with asthma, though. During an asthma attack or flare-up, the airways in the lungs become swollen. Muscles around the airways squeeze the bronchial tubes tight. The bronchial tubes make too much thick mucus. All this makes it hard for air to get through.

You can't stop yourself from getting asthma, but you can do a lot to control it.

What sets off an asthma flare-up? The answer is different for each person.

Ten-year-old Justin is allergic to cats. Petting a cat makes Justin's nose stuffy and his throat itchy. He starts to cough. If things get really bad, Justin has difficulty breathing. Cats are one of Justin's asthma **triggers**. Other common triggers may include
- a cold or **respiratory infection**
- allergies to mold, animals, dust, pollen, or cockroaches
- dirty, cold, or dry air
- exercise
- smoke or strong odors

Doctors can help asthmatics identify their triggers. By avoiding triggers, they have fewer and less severe flare-ups.

Each year asthma kills about 5,000 Americans. Good medical care could prevent many of these deaths.

Most asthmatics carry rescue inhalers.

There are two main types of asthma medications. Preventive medications are taken daily to prevent flare-ups. Rescue medications are taken during a flare-up to provide instant relief. These asthma medicines include

- **Anti-inflammatories** to reduce swelling
- Long-lasting **bronchodilators** to keep the squeezing muscles in the bronchi relaxed
- **Rescue inhalers** to loosen tight muscles to open airways for fast relief

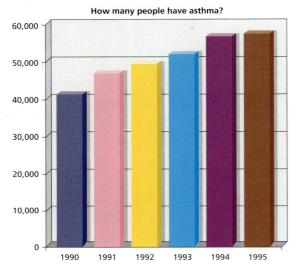

This six-year period shows the rise in asthma cases.

Asthma rates are increasing. Scientists aren't sure why. People of all ages and races get asthma, but these groups are more at risk:
- African Americans
- people who live in cities
- people with allergies
- people with a family history of asthma
- boys under the age of 12
- girls and women over the age of 12
- smokers and children whose parents smoke
- people who are overweight

Asthma and Athletics

Exercise is one of the main triggers of asthma. Exercise makes you breathe harder and faster, causing muscle spasms that tighten the bronchial tubes. Yet many top athletes have asthma. How do they combine superstar athletics with asthma?

It's all a matter of controlling the asthma. A doctor may prescribe a daily medicine to keep asthma flare-ups under control. Most athletes also keep a rescue inhaler handy so they can use it at the first sign of any asthma problems. Athletes with asthma don't have problems as long as they follow their programs of treatment.

Remember Jessica? Having asthma doesn't stop her from playing basketball. She follows a treatment plan created by her doctor. Jessica has good company. Some of the world's best athletes have asthma. As long as they stick with their treatments, though, asthma can't stop them.

Interview With

Jackie Joyner Kersee

Does asthma slow down Jackie Joyner Kersee? No way! This track-and-field superstar has six Olympic medals to prove it. In this question and answer session (Q & A), she talks about her asthma.

Q: Have you always had asthma?

A: I was nine when I started running, and I didn't notice it at the time. I was wheezing, but I was just used to breathing like that so I didn't realize anything was wrong. I didn't know until later that wheezing and shortness of breath is not normal.

Q: Has your asthma gotten worse or better?

A: Years ago it got worse because I wasn't treating it. Once I started to stick with the program [my doctor developed], though, I saw tremendous results. I got a lot better pretty fast and that has given me a lot of hope.

Now that she manages her asthma with a doctor's treatment plan, running is "no sweat" for Jackie Joyner Kersee.

NFL star running back Jerome Bettis is proof that asthma treatment works.

Other asthmatic athletes agree with Jackie that following a treatment plan is important. Swimmer Nancy Hogshead is a three-time Olympic gold medalist. She says, "PREVENT asthma! Don't wait until you're already sick before you start to take action."

NFL running back Jerome Bettis, named Pittsburgh Steeler's MVP twice, says, "I'm a real, breathing example of what people [with asthma] can do."

Tammy Jackson didn't win four WNBA championships with the Houston Comets by ignoring her asthma. "I never let asthma stop me from being the player I am," she insists.

Asthma is the last thing that's going to hold George Murray back. He is a world wheelchair marathon champion and the first person to cross the country in a wheelchair.

George Murray crossing the finish line

Nathalie C. K.

When Nathalie C. K. was six, she ended up in the emergency room with breathing difficulty. The diagnosis was an acute asthma attack.

A year later, Nathalie performed on stage at Radio City Music Hall, dancing next to actor Will Smith during the Grammy Awards.

Does all that dancing make Nathalie's asthma act up? "No," she says. "It's the opposite. Singing and dancing teaches me how to breathe better."

Living With Asthma

Having asthma used to mean there were things you couldn't do, like exercising strenuously or having certain pets. That isn't true anymore. As long as you take care of your asthma, you can do anything!

Today many doctors believe exercise can help asthmatics stay healthy. Children who are fit have less trouble with the disease—and more fun in life. There are even ways for people with pet allergies to deal with their asthma.

People who have asthma can take part in many activities.

Denise Pons with a furry friend

An animal shelter full of fluffy, furry, feathery critters is the last place you'd expect to find an asthmatic. The air in such a place is full of **allergens**. Denise Pons loves animals, though.

Denise has worked at the Animal Welfare League of Arlington, Virginia, for more than ten years. She trains volunteers, helps sick wildlife, and finds homes for pets.

Recently Denise discovered she had asthma. She learned that cats, bunnies, and hamsters are some of her triggers. Her doctor told her to quit her job and find new homes for her own dog and cat.

Quit working at the shelter? Give up her pets? No way! Instead Denise worked with her doctor on other ways to control her environment and to stop her flare-ups.

At home Denise banned Seamus the cat from her bedroom. Seamus and Sadie the dog started to get regular baths. Denise covered her sofas with blankets that can be removed and washed.

No matter what, Denise never goes to work without taking her asthma medication beforehand. She remembers to pack her rescue inhaler every day, too. She can't afford to get an asthma attack. After all, the animals count on her!

Interview With

Dr. Silverstein

Dr. Leonard Silverstein is an asthma and allergy specialist in New Jersey. In this Q & A he answers some questions many people have about asthma.

Q: Can asthmatics have furry pets?

A: It's probably best to avoid them, but it really depends on the results of a person's allergy testing.

Q: What is allergy testing?

A: There are some fairly easy tests to help figure out what triggers someone's asthma. For some people with allergies to dust or pollen, that's the trigger. For others, it may be a certain kind of animal they're allergic to.

Q: Are some animals better than others for people with asthma or allergies?

A: Well, if your allergy test shows that you're not allergic to dogs, then it's perfectly fine for you to have a dog. For someone who tests allergic, there are even some breeds of dogs that can be okay. We have to be more careful with cats. More people seem to be allergic to cats.

Q: Why is that?

A: We're not sure, but it has something to do with the cat **dander**. It is a much more common trigger with asthma.

Dog hair and dander under the microscope.

What the Future Holds

Today most asthmatics live active lives. Better medicines mean that living with asthma is easier than it was ten years ago.

Many asthmatics take medicine every day. Some, whose asthma is triggered by seasonal allergies, take it only during certain times of the year. These medicines help keep their airways open so they are less likely to get an asthma flare-up. Usually they also carry a rescue inhaler, just in case.

Keeping asthma under control, instead of waiting until it flares up, is the key to healthier living with asthma. What if asthma could be completely prevented, though?

Researchers think they may have found a **bacteria**—or microscopic germ—that may help. They are working on a **vaccine**, a shot that could keep you from getting asthma, but it's still too soon to say for sure.

Students at the Robert Poole Middle School in Baltimore use a special device to collect air quality information.

Fall is a tough time for asthmatic kids in Baltimore, Maryland. During October and November more kids in Baltimore visit hospitals with acute asthma attacks than at any other time of the year.

Scientists at NASA and the University of Maryland think air pollution could be to blame. Students and teachers at more than 20 Baltimore schools are helping them find out by collecting data on air quality.

It's important to eat healthy foods.

Could there be a link between asthma and what we eat? Researchers disagree about this. However, all doctors agree that eating a balanced diet is important to overall health. Some foods that may be helpful for asthmatics include vegetables, milk, fish, canola oil, and walnuts. Some doctors also suggest drinking plenty of water.

Asthma is a serious disease that is growing more common. You can help improve the lives of kids with asthma by
- showing your support for kids with asthma
- joining an anti-smoking campaign
- fighting air pollution
- learning all you can about asthma and sharing what you learn with others

Glossary

allergen — something that causes an allergic reaction such as coughing, sneezing or a rash

alveoli — tiny air sacs inside the lungs

anti-inflammatories — drugs that reduce swelling in the air tubes

asthmatic — a person with asthma

bacteria — living things that have one cell and can only be seen under a microscope

bronchial tubes — airways in the lungs

bronchodilators — medicines that help open the airways of the lungs, allowing more air to flow through them

dander — tiny pieces of hair, feather, or skin

rescue inhalers — medications that are inhaled with a special device and relax the airways

respiratory infection — a disease that affects the organs involved in breathing

trigger — something that causes asthma symptoms

vaccine — a substance put into the body to help fight off a disease

wheeze — to breathe with a raspy or whistling sound

Index

allergies 6, 15, 18–20
asthma attack 5, 14, 17, 21
at-risk groups 8
Bettis, Jerome 12
deaths 6
diet 22
exercise 6, 9, 15
flare-ups 6–7, 9, 17, 20
Hosghead, Nancy 12
Jackson, Tammy 13
Kersee, Jackie Joyner 10–11
medications, 7, 9, 20
Murray, George 13
pets 6, 15–19
pollution 21, 23
rates 8
rescue inhaler 7, 17, 20
triggers 6, 9, 17–20
vaccine 20

Book Treks 3	DRA™ Level	Guided Reading Level	Lexile Level
	38	P	760

Genre	Comprehension Skills and Strategies	Text Features	Content Connection
nonfiction: expository	• identifying cause and effect • identifying author's purpose	• table of contents • captions • bulleted list • diagram, labels • graph • subheads • glossary • index	science/ social studies

www.pearsonlearning.com

ISBN 0-7652-3002-X